Questions
for Couples
Journal

Questions to Enjoy, Reflect, and Connect with Your Partner

MAGGIE REYES

**ROCKRIDGE
PRESS**

Interior and Cover Designer: Jane Archer
Art Producer: Samantha Ulban
Editor: Lauren O'Neal
Illustrations © 2020 Anisa Makhoul.
Author photo courtesy of © Meivys Suarez

ISBN: Print 978-1-64611-952-3
R0

To my hubby, Mariano—

I want to know everything that is
knowable about you.

And to you, the readers—

may these questions bring you
closer together in love.

how to use this book

The most important thing to know about using this book is: **There is no wrong way to use this book.**

You can skip around and answer whatever questions call out to you in the moment, or you can start at the beginning and go through all the questions in order. You can designate someone to write down the answers, or you can each take turns. You can answer one question per day at a set time (such as at dinner or before bed), or you can go through several at once on a date night. You can even take this book with you on a road trip and play "getting to know you" as you drive toward a new adventure.

And of course, you can mix and match any of these ideas and add your own. What's important is that you have fun with it.

Questions are like portals to our hearts. In this journal, you have 400 of them. They're designed to be answered by you and your partner together, and every answer is meant to help you understand, love, and accept each other in a deeper way.

Using the power of these questions, you can...

✳ Spend quality time connecting with each other and igniting conversations that are meaningful and fun.

✳ Improve your communication in a way that feels safe and easy, and that allows you to better understand your partner in life and love.

✳ Learn more about each other's passions, dreams, and relationship goals, and brainstorm ideas about how to create a life together that you both love, whether you've been together for 30 days or 30 years.

There are seven categories of questions—some serious and deep, others lighthearted and entertaining. All the categories are varied throughout the book, so you'll have a bit of seriousness with a dash of fun as you read along. Each category will be color coded with its own special icon.

YOUR RELATIONSHIP
What is your relationship like with your partner? These questions explore the ins and outs of your relationship in the present—and how you envision it in the future.

GOALS AND DREAMS
These are questions about the things that inspire you and light you up as well as the things you're working toward in your life.

MEMORIES AND THE PAST

What made you who you are? These questions reflect on your formative experiences—both the victories and the difficulties. (Handle with extra care!)

VALUES AND BELIEFS

What's important to you? How do you experience the world? Learn more about your value system and core beliefs with these questions.

PASSION AND INTIMACY

Here we explore both the physical and emotional sides of sex. With these questions, set this intention: The closer you get to your partner, the more fun you'll have. If the word "intimacy" freaks you out a little, don't worry—for now, you can call it "sexy time" or anything else that feels more you.

COMMUNICATION

Are we going to talk about talking? We are! The questions here will also cover nonverbal communication—which, as we all know, can be the best kind.

JUST FOR FUN

You know those fun questions you see on social media, like "What was your favorite movie when you were 12?" Those types of questions will be in this category.

Remember, there is no wrong way to use this book—but there **is** a best way. The best way to use this book is to view these questions as an opportunity to **listen with an open heart.** Declare the time you spend answering these questions **a no-judgment zone** and practice being **honest, loving, and vulnerable** with each other.

Let's use the previous Just for Fun question as an example.

 What was your favorite movie when you were 12?

Star Wars: The Phantom Menace

Singin' in The Rain

An openhearted, no-judgment response would be: "That's fascinating! Why did you love it?"

A totally judgmental response would be: "Really? Of all the movies in the world, you picked **that** one?"

Do not do this. Ever. Period. Even for *The Phantom Menace.*

Here is why this is important: Judgment and criticism are relationship killers. Humans are hardwired to seek safety and avoid danger, and because judgment and criticism represent danger to the human brain, any answer you criticize will make your partner's brain shut down. Your partner will freeze and not want to continue.

Conversely, when you practice openhearted curiosity, you'll help make your partner feel safe. This increases the likelihood that they'll want to share more.

If you do have an intense reaction to one of your partner's responses, the best thing to do is pause, take a slow, deep breath to relax your nervous system, and get curious. Curiosity is like fertilizer—it will always make your relationship stronger and help it grow.

So remember:
Openhearted curiosity—**YES.**
Judgment and criticism—**NO.**

Now enjoy learning more about yourself, your partner, and your relationship with these 400 questions.

What about your partner inspired you to want to get to know them better when you first met?

Describe your dream house. Is it big or small? In a city or somewhere rural?

What is the first trip you
remember taking as a kid?

What is a hobby you wish you had time for?

What is one of your favorite ways to show physical affection to your partner?

What is different about your relationship with your partner than other relationships you've had in the past?

You get to spend a week with someone you admire in sports, entertainment, science, politics, or the arts. Who do you choose, and what do you do together?

What is an activity you loved growing up that you would want to share with your partner now?

If your partner is getting you a gift, would you prefer to help pick it out or to be completely surprised?

Your birthday is declared a national holiday! What is the official meal of that holiday?

What does "teamwork" in a relationship mean to you?

Does your current job inspire you or cause you stress? Or both?

What are some things you and your partner can do together to create more good memories than bad ones?

Do you think flirting with your partner matters in a long-term relationship? Why or why not?

How often should you and your partner check in with each other every day?

 What is something you and your partner haven't done yet that you're excited about doing together?

What are three cities you would love to visit? What appeals to you about them?

_____

_____

_____

_____

_____

_____

_____

_____

_____

While growing up, what did money mean to you? What does it mean to you now?

_____

_____

_____

_____

_____

_____

_____

_____

_____

_____

What is more valuable to you: a $10,000 increase in pay or an extra week off and no late hours?

What is one of your favorite sexual memories with your partner?

In relationships, do you consider yourself a risk-taker, or are you risk averse?

How much money would you like to have saved up at the end of the year? How about in five years?

Are you still in touch with your childhood friends?

We make decisions, both big and small, every day. Which ones do you involve your partner in and why?

If you could go back to school and excel at one subject, which subject would you pick? Why?

When you and your partner's schedules are hectic, how can you ensure that you spend time together as partners and have regular date nights?

What is a goal or a dream you had in the past that you regret not pursuing? Do you have an interest in pursuing it now?

Did you have any special or unique bedtime rituals as a kid?

To be the best partner possible, what new experiences are you willing to try?

_____

_____

_____

_____

_____

_____

_____

_____

_____

What is one rule about communicating that you can promise your partner you'll follow?

_____

_____

_____

_____

_____

_____

_____

_____

_____

How do you think you and your partner should handle holidays with your loved ones?

_____

_____

_____

_____

_____

_____

_____

_____

_____

_____

 How can you ensure sex remains a priority in your relationship?

_____

_____

_____

_____

_____

_____

_____

_____

_____

_____

Would you rather spend money on a big vacation or save for a dream house? (Check one.)

▓ Big vacation all the way!

▓ A dream house is forever.

▓ Big vacation all the way!

▓ A dream house is forever.

If you could time travel, would you go back into the past or forward into the future? (Circle one.)

PAST   FUTURE

PAST   FUTURE

Which will get you further in life: book smarts or street smarts?

What is the role of spirituality or faith in your relationship with your partner?

What is one feeling you'd love to experience every day?

Name one thing about your childhood that felt hard and one thing that felt easy.

_____

_____

_____

_____

_____

_____

_____

_____

 If you and your partner both contribute to your relationship based on your strengths, what are some ways you could balance your contributions?

_____

_____

_____

_____

_____

_____

_____

_____

_____

If you and your partner chose your own Secret Service code names, what would they be?

When you think about your future together, what worries you the most?

Success is built on a mountain of failures. How can you support each other when one of you encounters failure?

What did you learn about taking risks versus playing it safe when you were growing up?

What is your favorite piece of furniture? Why do you love it?

How do you feel you learn best: by having things explained out loud or through visual and written examples?

On a scale of 1 to 10, how would you rate the quality of your friendship with your partner right now? What would help raise that number?

What is your dream car?

Did you win any awards as a kid?
What were they?

Should personal ethics ever be compromised for
the greater good?

What is your favorite time of day to have sex?

If you and your partner took a cooking class, what would you love to learn how to make?

When you achieve a goal, what's a meaningful way to celebrate?

What is your favorite holiday memory from childhood?

In what part of your life do you feel the most confident? In what part do you feel the most insecure?

_____

_____

_____

_____

_____

_____

_____

_____

_____

You can either go to space for one day or travel on a world cruise for a whole year. Which one do you choose?

_____

_____

_____

_____

_____

_____

_____

_____

If a boundary needs to be set with a family member and your partner is uncomfortable setting that boundary, how can you approach it as a team?

 Think of a dream you have right now. What are you willing and unwilling to give up to achieve it?

Who was your favorite fictional character growing up?

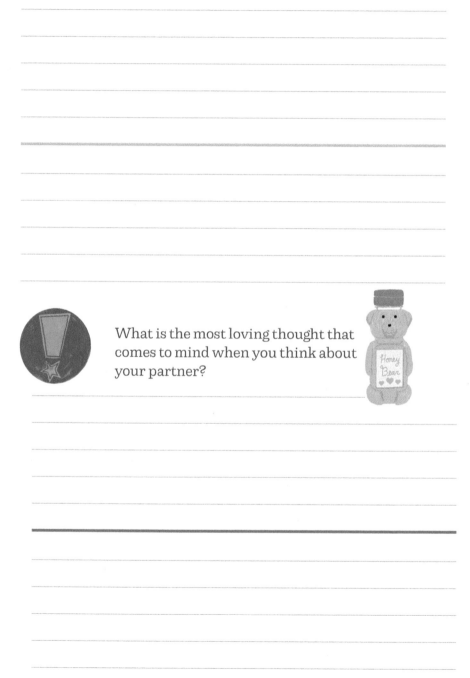

What is the most loving thought that comes to mind when you think about your partner?

If you felt your partner didn't need to understand everything about you in order to love you, how would that affect your communication?

What is a daily habit that will help you achieve your dream?

I think public displays of affection are fun and romantic, and I enjoy them. (Circle one.)

YES   NO

YES   NO

You have the opportunity to take a dream trip somewhere your partner has no interest in visiting. Do you go without your partner? (Circle one.)

YES   NO

YES   NO

Music was better when I was growing up than it is now. (Circle one.)

TRUE   FALSE

TRUE   FALSE

What are three words you would use to describe your favorite qualities about your partner?

What is your favorite way to relax?

Imagine that five people you've always wanted to meet are waiting to play a game with you. Who are the five people? What game do you play?

What is the biggest obstacle you and your partner need to overcome to have a thriving relationship?

When achieving a goal becomes challenging, what motivates you to keep going?

Before you met your partner, what did you think about relationships? What do you think about them now?

Do you currently contribute money to any charities? If so, which ones, and why did you choose them?

What is one tip you'd give your partner on how to best communicate with you?

What song would you pick to describe your relationship with your partner, and why?

 When you think about having fun with your partner, do you like to plan ahead or be spontaneous?

If you were raised by more than one parent or guardian, how do you think their relationship has affected your current relationship?

When you get stressed out, what is something you tend to do that you would like to either stop doing or do less of?

What do you think about monogamy?

_____

_____

_____

_____

_____

_____

_____

_____

_____

What do you remember about the first time you met your partner?

_____

_____

_____

_____

_____

_____

_____

_____

_____

_____

What is the biggest fear you've had to overcome to achieve a goal?

 What is a fun adventure from your past that you love to remember?

Think about your last disagreement with your partner. What is one specific way you could handle it better next time?

You and your partner get to enter the world of one of your favorite movies for a week. What movie world do you want to live in for that week?

Complete this sentence: "The secret to a thriving relationship is . . ."

_____

_____

_____

_____

_____

_____

_____

_____

How do you know when it's time to try harder to achieve a goal versus when it's time to focus on a new one?

_____

_____

_____

_____

_____

_____

_____

_____

_____

What is one thing you want your partner to know about your past that will help them love you better in the present?

If you got an offer for a dream job but it required you to move, what would make you consider moving?

On which parts of your body do you love being kissed?

Think of a favorite TV show you and your partner like to watch together. What makes watching it together fun?

If you had to pick a dream you could only begin to pursue once you turn 60, what would you choose and why?

What is your favorite memory from a birthday celebration when you were growing up? What made it special?

What type of work is most meaningful to you?

What is a nonverbal action that immediately communicates love to you?

On a scale of 1 to 5, with 1 being "I like to let life surprise me" and 5 being "Goal Crusher is my middle name," how important is goal-setting to you? (Circle a number.)

1   2   3   4   5

1   2   3   4   5

You receive your dream car as a gift. Do you keep it or trade it in and use the money for something else? (Check one.)

☐ Keep the car!

☐ Trade it in and buy _____ instead.

☐ Keep the car!

☐ Trade it in and buy _____ instead.

Name one thing that is easy for you but often hard for other people.

_____   _____

When you're upset, would you
prefer your partner give you space
or stay with you until you calm down?

If you could meet one person who could help you
achieve one of your dreams, who would you want
to meet and what help would you seek from them?

If you could have a closing ceremony or special ritual to mark the end of a chapter in your past, what chapter would it be?

Twenty years from now, when you look back at your relationship with your partner, what would make you consider it a great success?

Your partner comes home from a long trip, and you can use only physical affection to show how much you've missed them. What do you do?

_____

_____

_____

_____

_____

_____

_____

_____

_____

Would you prefer several smaller vacations with your partner throughout the year or one epic vacation that you look forward to all year long?

_____

_____

_____

_____

_____

_____

_____

Is your approach to planning for the future similar to your partner's or different? How so?

What is a memory of your partner that inspires you to love them even more whenever you think about it?

Many companies have a "corporate culture" that reflects their values. How would you describe the "relationship culture" you have with your partner?

What does "openhearted listening" mean to you? Use at least three adjectives to describe it.

What is one thing you'd regret never doing with your partner?

Have you ever had a dream come true, only to find it wasn't anything like you'd expected? What did you learn?

What were your weekends like as a kid?

When you've made a mistake and want to make it up to your partner, what is the kindest thing you can do for them?

Growing up, what was one belief you had about sex that you no longer have?

 What are some activities you and your partner can plan that would make for reliably fun date nights?

You win the lottery and can build your dream house anywhere in the world, but it can't be in the area you currently live in. Where do you move and why?

What are three things you're proud of accomplishing in your life so far?

Have you ever been afraid to share your point of view for fear of rejection?

You get free tickets to see your three favorite musical artists, but you get to meet only one of them. Who are the three artists playing and which one do you meet?

Can you love your partner without trying to change them? Does this feel easy or hard?

What is your ideal retirement? Where would you live? How would you spend your time?

Who was the first person you told when you knew your partner was The One? What did you say about your partner?

_____

_____

_____

_____

_____

_____

_____

_____

What is your preferred strategy for dealing with a difficult person?

_____

_____

_____

_____

_____

_____

_____

_____

_____

_____

Circle the one quality you most want to embody for your partner:

Loving   Patient   Passionate

Devoted   Loyal   Committed

Loving   Patient   Passionate

Devoted   Loyal   Committed

Name your biggest celebrity crush when you were growing up.

_____ _____

On a scale of 1 to 10, where 1 is "not important at all" and 10 is "super important," how important is it for you and your partner to share thoughts and feelings regularly? (Circle one.)

1   2   3   4   5   6   7   8   9   10

---

1   2   3   4   5   6   7   8   9   10

What do you and your partner love the most about spending time together?

What is a daily habit that might be keeping you from making progress on a goal right now? Are you willing to give up that habit?

When you were a child, what would make you jump out of bed excited for the day?

 What do you believe is the role of pleasure in your life and in your relationship with your partner?

What is one thing that gets you excited and makes you feel sexy, and one thing that is a total mood killer?

_____

_____

_____

_____

_____

_____

_____

_____

_____

 What is one thing you'd love to ask for in your relationship with your partner but are scared to talk about? Why does it scare you?

_____

_____

_____

_____

_____

_____

_____

_____

_____

What are three physical things and three emotional things you always want in your home?

Is there any addiction in your family? How did you cope with it growing up?

If you look back at all the things you did yesterday, how did you make sure your schedule matched your priorities? What would you do differently?

If you could be the world champion of anything, what would it be?

Are you an introvert (need quiet time alone to recharge) or an extrovert (need lots of people around to recharge)? How do you think that affects your relationship with your partner?

Have you ever felt compelled to pursue a goal someone else wanted for you?

What was your favorite gift you ever received as a kid? What is your favorite gift you've received as an adult?

 What delights you the most about your relationship with your partner?

Are you a "give me the bottom line and just stick to the facts" kind of person or a "start at the beginning and tell me all the details" kind of person?

What is something you and your partner haven't done in a while that you want to make time for soon?

Complete this sentence: "My purpose in life is …"

 What were you afraid of in the past that you're no longer afraid of now?

What is an important value you'd like to prioritize more this year? How would you know at the end of the year that you prioritized it?

Would you be willing to try something outside your comfort zone sexually? Why or why not?

What does your partner need to know in order to support you when you're upset?

_____

_____

_____

_____

_____

_____

_____

_____

_____

_____

If our thoughts influence our behaviors, what is the most useful thought you can have about a goal you're working toward?

_____

_____

_____

_____

_____

_____

_____

_____

_____

What is something you loved doing as a kid that you still love doing now?

_____

_____

_____

_____

_____

_____

_____

_____

_____

How do you currently manage stress? What are some things you do to calm down when you feel "fight, flight, or freeze" coming on?

_____

_____

_____

_____

_____

_____

_____

_____

You can choose any job you want, and you'll be paid well every year for doing it, but you have to do it for 20 years. What job do you choose?

 What are three aspects of your relationship that you love?

What is one of your financial dreams (e.g., buying a house, paying off student loan debt)?

Think of a role model you had growing up. Why did you look up to them?

What are important factors you take into consideration when deciding where to live?

Emotional safety is the foundation of communication. What is one thing you can do to help your partner feel safe enough to open up to you?

What is something you loved about your partner when you met that you love even more now?

What personal goals do you want to share with other people? What personal goals do you want to keep between you and your partner?

Did you play with board games, puzzles, or cards as a kid? What were your favorites?

 What are three things that you think are important to spend money on?

What is something sexual you would love to try with your partner?

_____

_____

_____

_____

_____

_____

_____

_____

_____

What makes an apology meaningful to you?

_____

_____

_____

_____

_____

_____

_____

_____

_____

_____

Sometimes people fear losing their partners if a big dream comes true, so they avoid pursuing it. Have you ever felt that way?

What did you think about romantic love when you were growing up?

What are your thoughts about combining finances and sharing the money you and your partner make? How do you determine an equitable distribution?

Your life story is being made into a TV show. What is it called? Who plays you? Who plays your partner?

What helps you relax emotionally and feel safe to open up? How can your partner contribute to those feelings of safety and relaxation?

What is one of your favorite goals or dreams you decided to go for and ultimately achieved? Looking back, how does it feel to know you succeeded?

When you were growing up, did you tend to meet challenges head-on or avoid dealing with them?

What do you think is the most important quality a good partner can have? How do you try to embody this quality yourself?

What is one thing you can stop doing with your body language or tone that will help you communicate more lovingly with your partner?

How would you define being a great partner in this relationship?

If you and your partner could prioritize only one of these this year, which would it be? (Circle one)

Saving money

Eating healthier

Physical fitness

Decluttering our living space

Other: _____
_____

Saving money

Eating healthier

Physical fitness

Decluttering our living space

Other: _____

On a scale of 1 to 10, how excited were you when you first got your driver's license? (Circle one.)

1 2 3 4 5 6 7 8 9 10
_____

1 2 3 4 5 6 7 8 9 10

Do you prefer to be spontaneous or plan ahead? (Check one.)

▢ Surprise me!   ▢ Give me the plan!
_____

▢ Surprise me!   ▢ Give me the plan!

Do you feel that you and your partner are currently striking a good balance between being a team and leading independent lives?

How do you stay focused on your top priorities?

Is there something from your past that your partner has helped you heal from?

What is a personal strength you have worked hard to cultivate?

Many experts suggest that scheduling sex helps you have it more often. What are your thoughts about this?

_____

_____

_____

_____

_____

_____

_____

_____

What makes you feel closest to your partner?

_____

_____

_____

_____

_____

_____

_____

_____

Do you or your partner have a dream you are reluctant to pursue? What makes you hesitate?

Who was your favorite teacher in school, and why?

What specific words or gestures make for a good apology?

You and your partner are granted one wish together, but you have to invent a plausible cover story to explain it to everyone else. What's the wish? The story?

What has surprised you the most about
your partner?

_____

_____

_____

_____

_____

_____

_____

_____

_____

_____

_____

 What is a hobby of yours that, if given the chance,
you would love to get paid to do for a living?

_____

_____

_____

_____

_____

_____

_____

_____

_____

_____

_____

If you could turn back the clock to any point in time, what year would you choose and why?

How often do you like to spend time with your extended family?

What is one emotion that makes it difficult for you to communicate clearly and effectively?

_____

_____

_____

_____

_____

_____

_____

_____

_____

What is the role of acceptance in a healthy relationship?

_____

_____

_____

_____

_____

_____

_____

_____

_____

What is your favorite way to use money (e.g., giving to charity, shopping)?

 What is something that happened in your past that was hard to forgive?

What is the best way to end an argument?

What is the sexiest part of your partner's body to you? Why do you love it?

What are three simple things you and your partner do to keep your relationship strong?

What are some fun activities you can do as a couple to maintain your physical health?

What is a memory from a trip with your partner that still makes you laugh whenever you think about it?

In a typical day, how many hours should you and your partner spend together, and how much time should be scheduled to pursue individual interests?

You are given $10,000 to spend every day for the next five days. You can't save it, and the money does not carry over. What do you buy?

_____

_____

_____

_____

_____

_____

_____

_____

 How do you and your partner currently handle criticism from others? Moving forward, what might be a more productive way to handle it?

_____

_____

_____

_____

_____

_____

_____

_____

_____

_____

How do you balance a sense of urgency about achieving a dream with spending fulfilling and enjoyable days with your partner?

 What is a hobby or pastime you love doing with your partner? What makes it fun?

Which is sexiest? (Check one.)

☐ A quiet night at home

☐ A night away in a fancy hotel

☐ Camping under the stars

☐ Other: _____

☐ A quiet night at home

☐ A night away in a fancy hotel

☐ Camping under the stars

☐ Other: _____

Which is more important when it comes to solving problems: creativity or methodical analysis? (Circle one.)

Creativity   Methodical analysis

Creativity   Methodical analysis

What was your favorite subject in high school?

_____   _____

If you could guarantee that one of your partner's dreams would come true, which one would you choose and why?

What is something you're holding on to right now that you know you need to give up if you want to make space for more happiness?

Do you ever regret actions you take when you're angry? What would help you when you feel overwhelmed by anger in the future?

What quality do you think is most useful to practice during difficult conversations?

What does your partner need to know about you to love you better?

_____

_____

_____

_____

_____

_____

_____

_____

_____

In general, are you eager or hesitant to try new things?

_____

_____

_____

_____

_____

_____

_____

_____

_____

What is a hobby you tried and found out you didn't enjoy?

What do you need to believe about yourself to feel more sexually confident?

What is one small thing you can do to cultivate good will and friendship with your partner every day?

 Name something that once felt like a faraway dream but eventually happened. How did you feel when it came true?

What was the most recent thing your partner did or said that made you laugh?

How important do you believe money is to happiness? What amount of money feels like "enough"?

You get to create a reality show about any topic. What is it about, and what do you name it? Are you and your partner cast members?

Which chores do you actually kind of like?

What activities put you in a "flow state," where it feels like time expands or stands still and you lose yourself in the moment?

What do you remember or know about your great-grandparents?

What favors do you enjoy doing for your partner?

_____

_____

_____

_____

_____

_____

_____

_____

_____

Cars need preventive maintenance and tune-ups. How can you apply that idea to your communication with your partner?

_____

_____

_____

_____

_____

_____

_____

_____

_____

_____

What changes, if any, should you and your partner make when it comes to how you handle money together?

 How would you like your partner to support you when a goal or dream feels hard?

What is one event in your past that you wish you could do over?

Do you stay in touch with any of your past bosses? Why or why not?

Name one way you could be creative about initiating sex with your partner.

_____

_____

_____

_____

_____

_____

_____

_____

_____

_____

 When it comes to planning time together with your partner, do you prefer lots of activities, lots of downtime, or a mix?

_____

_____

_____

_____

_____

_____

_____

_____

_____

_____

_____

How involved should you be with the goals and dreams of the people you care about? What do you want to give, and what are your limits?

Name two things about your past that you're grateful for.

What is something you find difficult? What would make it easier?

You get to pick one thing from your favorite store that you never have to pay for again. What do you choose?

When you think about boundaries (what's okay and not okay for you), what's the easiest boundary for you to set?

_____

_____

_____

_____

_____

_____

_____

_____

_____

What is one success you had in the past that makes you more confident in pursuing goals in the present?

_____

_____

_____

_____

_____

_____

_____

_____

_____

What helped you feel safe as a child? What helps you feel safe now?

 What is the most "valuable" thing you own? Is it a physical object or something else?

Name one way you can make your everyday conversations with your partner more fun.

_____

_____

_____

_____

_____

_____

_____

_____

_____

Why do you think relationships sometimes grow stale? How can you avoid this in your own relationship?

_____

_____

_____

_____

_____

_____

_____

_____

_____

How do you decide when it's time to reassess a goal?

 Which holiday did you most look forward to when you were growing up? Is it still your favorite?

Describe your family in three words.

What is a fun sexual fantasy you'd love to share with your partner? Why is it fun to you?

What should the role of technology be in the time and spaces you share with your partner? When and how often should you put your devices away?

 What is one task that, if you never had to do it again, would feel like a dream come true?

What was your favorite team sport growing up?
Did you like to play it, watch it, or both?

What are the top two or three qualities you look
for in friends?

You get to play only one board game for the rest of your life. What game do you pick and why?

_____

_____

_____

_____

_____

_____

_____

_____

_____

_____

Do you struggle with any habits, emotions, or past experiences that could affect the quality of your relationship with your partner?

_____

_____

_____

_____

_____

_____

_____

_____

_____

_____

What is a dream so big it feels hard to say it out loud, but it would be amazing if it came true?

What was your favorite book that you had to read for school and actually enjoyed?

When you have a stressful day, what is one way your partner can support you and offer you comfort?

Name one thing you can do during or right after an argument if you want the experience to bring you closer together instead of further apart.

How should you and your partner split up chores? How often should you check in and make tweaks to this setup?

What does success mean to you?

If your adult self could go back and give your child self a pep talk, what would you say?

Name your top three personal values.

You plan a secret, sexy getaway for you and your partner. Where do you take them? Describe the romantic details you would add to the trip.

What is your favorite way to stay connected with your partner when you're traveling or away from each another for an extended period of time?

How often should you and your partner check in about your current goals? Should you schedule it or just talk informally now and then?

 Did you have any hobbies as a kid? What were they?

If you were guaranteed success either way, would you rather work at a startup or a 100-year-old company?

Your favorite deli names a sandwich after you. What are the ingredients, and what is it called?

What do you think is a good balance between routine and excitement in a relationship?

How can you plan to stay connected to your partner when you're working toward a goal that might require extra hours apart?

Would you like to share a difficult memory from your past? (It doesn't have to be the darkest one— just something that might help your partner understand you.)

How often do you spend time thinking about and planning for your future?

In which situations is it easiest for you to communicate clearly? In which situations is it hardest?

 What is a simple and fun way you and your partner could show love to each other?

When pursuing a dream, is it important to enjoy the process, or are you mostly focused on the end result?

What were you taught about religion growing up? How does that impact your spirituality today?

What is your favorite store or place to shop?

 How often should you and your partner discuss money and finances?

Name one thing that always helps you feel sexier.

_____   _____

 The place I often get stuck when I am trying to communicate is . . . (Check one.)

▨ Listening without taking it personally

▨ Clearly conveying what I'm thinking and wanting

▨ Other: _____

▨ Listening without taking it personally

▨ Clearly conveying what I'm thinking and wanting

▨ Other: _____

 You and your partner are given everything you need to start a business together, but you must personally run it for the next five years and you can pick from only these two choices. (Check one.)

▨ International space station   ▨ Bakery

▨ International space station   ▨ Bakery

What is your favorite gift that your partner has ever given you?

_____

_____

_____

_____

_____

_____

_____

_____

Have you ever had a big dream that didn't come true? How did that affect you? How do you think about it now?

_____

_____

_____

_____

_____

_____

_____

_____

_____

What did you do when you got angry as a kid? What do you do now?

 What is a good habit you'd like to practice when it comes to managing money wisely?

If you fully unleashed your sexual self, what (if anything) would be different about your sex life now?

When you think about the different challenges you've had in life, what is one that has made you a better partner?

When focusing on a goal, do you tend to "work harder" or look for shortcuts to "work smarter"?

What is the best advice you have ever received?

Think about one of the most thoughtful things your partner has ever done for you. Why is it meaningful to you?

 You win free vacations for the next five years, but you have to go to the same place every time. What place do you choose?

If one partner makes more money than the other, how should both partners approach investing financially in the relationship?

 What is one personal weakness you feel you need to overcome to achieve your biggest dream?

What's a quote you remember from your past that still inspires you today?

What do you value more: ambition (striving for more in life) or contentment (savoring what you have in life)?

What is something that, if practiced regularly, would make most of your conversations with your partner easier?

_____

_____

_____

_____

_____

_____

_____

_____

_____

What do you miss most about being single? What tweaks can you make to include any part of that in your relationship now?

_____

_____

_____

_____

_____

_____

_____

_____

_____

Name three things that would be happening often in your ideal home life (e.g., sit-down dinners, game nights).

When you were a child, what scared you the most?

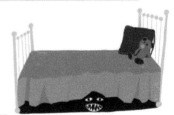

Do you ever find it difficult to say no to things you don't want to do? How do you handle it?

Name the wackiest code word or code phrase for sex that would make you laugh every time you heard it.

How can having clear boundaries make your relationship with your partner stronger?

What was the last detour or distraction that slowed you down when trying to achieve a goal?

What is something that used to cause you stress in your past but doesn't anymore?

What is one thing that would contribute to making your relationship feel good regularly?

You get paid to take a year off to write a book about any topic. What do you write about?

How can you and your partner honor each other's eating preferences and values when dining together?

What is one goal you would like to achieve in the next three months? What is one goal you would like to achieve in the next three years?

What is one skill you learned from your parent(s) or guardian(s) that you find helpful in your relationship now?

What are some words you and your partner should say to each other as often as possible?

What is the hardest topic for you to bring up to your partner? How could you make it easier to talk about?

If you had to issue a report card for the state of your relationship as it is today, what grade would you give it? Why? What grade would you like it to be?

Psychologists say that feeling like we're contributing to something bigger than ourselves makes us happier than money. Do you agree?

What were your favorite foods as a kid? What foods did you absolutely refuse to eat?

_____

_____

_____

_____

_____

_____

_____

_____

_____

How do you feel about investing in continuing education (getting a master's, taking professional development classes, etc.)?

_____

_____

_____

_____

_____

_____

_____

_____

What is your favorite sexy or romantic movie?

_____   _____

Would you rather have $100 million or one super-power for the rest of your life? (Check one.)

▨ More money, honey!   ▨ Power me up!

▨ More money, honey!   ▨ Power me up!

Talking about sex with my partner is easy for me. (Circle one.)

TRUE   FALSE

TRUE   FALSE

What is one thing in your relationship that would become easier if you let go of your expectations of how it should be and just accepted it for what it is?

 What is a simple thing that can help you feel happier today, regardless of what the future holds?

Which holiday rituals and celebrations do you want to re-create with your partner? Which do you want to leave behind?

What are two ways you and your partner can practice gratitude regularly?

You get to plan the ultimate date night. Where do you go, and what do you do?

If one of you has a hobby or passion the other isn't interested in, how do you both handle it?

You and your partner feel certain about achieving a big goal together. What do you do tomorrow to influence the positive outcome of that goal?

What is a place you've been to without your partner that you'd love to take them to?

What kinds of animals do you have or want as pets? How many?

When you're having a disagreement, what is a code word or phrase that would (a) indicate you need to take a break, and (b) make you smile?

Who were or are your role models for healthy relationships? What can you learn from them?

_____

_____

_____

_____

_____

_____

_____

_____

_____

What is a goal you're working on right now that you would regret not accomplishing if you don't stick to it?

_____

_____

_____

_____

_____

_____

_____

_____

_____

What's the best gift you've ever given someone else?

There's a saying that some people work to live, while others live to work. Which one do you identify with more?

Imagine you're a superhero. What superpowers do you have? What is your origin story?

_____

_____

_____

_____

_____

_____

_____

_____

_____

_____

Should you and your partner share passwords with each other? Why or why not?

_____

_____

_____

_____

_____

_____

_____

_____

_____

_____

What are three of your greatest strengths that are helpful when working toward a goal?

How do you know when you have truly forgiven someone?

What is your favorite lesson you've learned in life
so far? How have you changed as a result?

Think of someone you know who is
a really good listener. What makes
them a good listener?

Besides your relationship with your partner, what is one of the most important relationships in your life?

What are your top three priorities in life right now?

When you were younger, what scared you the most about becoming an adult?

_____

_____

_____

_____

_____

_____

_____

_____

_____

 If you ask your partner to do something they're not good at and they fail, what can you do or say to help them feel better?

_____

_____

_____

_____

_____

_____

_____

_____

_____

If you could invent an award for something and name it, what would you call it?

_____

_____

_____

_____

_____

_____

_____

_____

 Do you think you and your partner have a similar approach to saving and spending money?

_____

_____

_____

_____

_____

_____

_____

_____

_____

What are your thoughts about asking for help with achieving your dreams?

_____

_____

_____

_____

_____

_____

_____

_____

Is apologizing easy or difficult for you?

_____

_____

_____

_____

_____

_____

_____

_____

Were special occasions stressful or fun growing up? Were they a mix of both?

When you're passionate about a topic, do you find it easier or harder to discuss that topic?

What is the most important thing you want from a relationship? How can you and your partner prioritize each other's "most important thing"?

What is your ideal work schedule? What would need to happen in your work life to get closer to that ideal schedule?

You are packing for a sexy trip with your partner. List three things you would bring.

 What is the role of forgiveness in a healthy relationship?

What do you value more: freedom or security?

_____

_____

_____

_____

_____

_____

_____

_____

_____

What is one major life-changing event that helped shape who you are today?

_____

_____

_____

_____

_____

_____

_____

_____

_____

_____

_____

How can you and your partner help each other make difficult decisions, especially if those decisions could disappoint others?

 Are you still excited by your current life goals? Why or why not?

What is one thing you have always done when your feelings are hurt but that you would like to stop doing in order to become a better partner?

What is something you've done in your relationship that you wish you could take back and do over?

If you could give a speech on a cause you're passionate about at the United Nations, what would that cause be?

Name at least three qualities you want to display as a partner.

Describe a "dream" day—a day that would be so fun you would consider it a dream come true.

_____

_____

_____

_____

_____

_____

_____

_____

_____

_____

Name one of your favorite memories that you and your partner have made together so far.

_____

_____

_____

_____

_____

_____

_____

_____

_____

_____

What is one of the boldest things you've ever done? What did you learn from it?

What is your favorite way to initiate sex?

What could you teach someone looking for examples of a healthy relationship?

_____

_____

_____

_____

_____

_____

_____

_____

_____

Is one of your current goals in life to feel closer and more connected with your partner? Why or why not?

_____

_____

_____

_____

_____

_____

_____

_____

_____

What was your favorite after-school snack when you were a kid?

If you had a motto or slogan for your life, what would it be?

You are allowed to travel to the future and bring one sentence of information back to the present. What would that sentence be?

_____

_____

_____

_____

_____

_____

_____

_____

_____

 What is your biggest fear about your current relationship, and how can you make it smaller?

_____

_____

_____

_____

_____

_____

_____

_____

_____

_____

_____

What advice were you given about sex growing up? Did any of it turn out to be good advice?

What are your favorite words of wisdom to give?

What is one quality you can improve on to become a better listener?

 Name one situation in which you always want to check with your partner first to make sure you're working as a team.

Imagine you've achieved your most important goal. What's different about your life, and what's the same?

 What did your family or guardians teach you about what love looks like?

What kinds of situations make you anxious?

 What is one of your favorite things your partner does to show you physical affection?

If you could learn any language in the world, what would it be? Why?

How does it affect your relationship when you don't regularly spend time with your partner?

What do you think is the role of grit and persistence in achieving goals?

What emotion felt overwhelming when you were growing up? How do you manage that feeling now?

If you had to describe your relationship with your partner in one sentence, how would you describe it?

 You get to invent your own lottery. You can give away anything—except money. What do you give away?

When it comes to sharing details about your relationship on social media, what would you consider okay, and what would you consider not okay?

What is something you believe to be a waste of time but do anyway? Why do you still do it?

What is your favorite
memory of being out in nature
or enjoying the outdoors?

If you could go back and give yourself advice
during a painful chapter in your life, what would it
be?

Is it easier to talk about money with your partner than with others?

If you and your partner each think you're right about something, how can you remind each other to be open to new perspectives?

What is your biggest dream
for your relationship?

 What is something in your past you're proud of accomplishing that has helped you become a better partner now?

What are some qualities a great leader
should have?

What goals do you want to set with your partner
when it comes to sex?

If you had an Emergency Relationship Resuscitation Plan, what would you include in it?

 What is one realistic goal you're working toward right now? What's one goal that feels more like a dream but you're working toward it anyway?

What is an experience from your past that both feels hard to talk about and has an impact on how you relate to your partner today?

What does generosity mean to you?

What is one of the silliest things you've ever done?

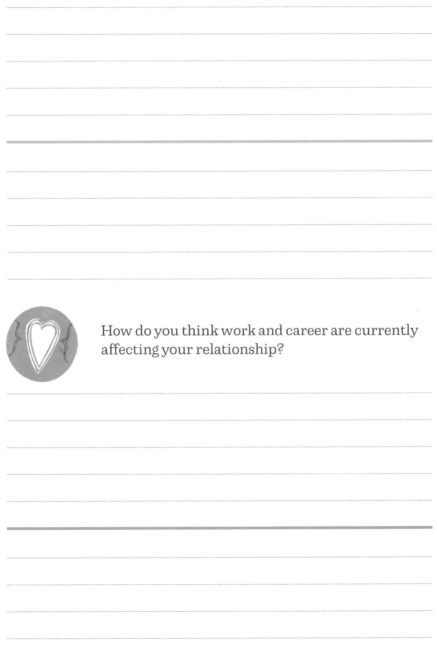 How do you think work and career are currently affecting your relationship?

What is something you want to accomplish in the next year? How can your partner support you with that goal?

Thinking about all the friends you've had throughout your life, what makes a friend "good"?

What are the three most essential principles that guide your life?

 Is it okay to bring up the past in arguments? Why or why not?

Name one thing you do often in your relationship that you're really proud of.

_____

_____

_____

_____

_____

_____

_____

_____

_____

What is one thing that always reminds you of a happy memory from your past?

_____

_____

_____

_____

_____

_____

_____

_____

_____

_____

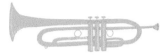 What do you most want your partner to know about you?

 Your relationship with your partner is made into a trilogy. What is the name of the final installment?